ICOPROMO – Intercultural competence for professional mobility

Evelyne Glaser
Manuela Guilherme
María del Carmen Méndez García
Terry Mughan

With support from:
Mike Byram
Duarte Silva
Anne Sofia Holmberg
Marisa María Luisa Pérez Cañado
Alexandra Kaar
Iris Fischlmayr
Olga Arcalá Campillo
Jelena Jefimova
Clara Keating
Daniel Hoppe
Marcus Abílio Pereira
Vivien Burrows

European Centre for Modern Languages

Council of Europe Publishing

French edition:

Compétence interculturelle pour le développement de la mobilité professionnelle
ISBN: 978-92-871-6142-0

The opinions expressed in this publication are not to be regarded as reflecting the policy of any government, of the Committee of Ministers or of the Secretary General of the Council of Europe.

Cover: Gross Werbeagentur, Graz
Printer: Bachernegg, Kapfenberg
Layout: Christian Stenner, Graz

http://book.coe.int
Council of Europe Publishing
F-67075 Strasbourg Cedex

European Centre for Modern Languages / Council of Europe
Nikolaiplatz 4
A-8020 Graz
Austria
www.ecml.at

ISBN: 978-92-871-6143-7
© Council of Europe, 2007

Acknowledgements

We are grateful to the ECML and the Council of Europe for granting us the opportunity to work on this fascinating topic, and the ECML staff in Graz for their expert advice and for providing a truly supportive and inspiring intellectual environment during our meetings.

We would also like to thank AVL List GmbH and GIBS (Graz International Bilingual School) for hosting a group of workshop participants and for allowing them to carry out an ethnographic activity for the ICOPROMO project on their premises.

We are greatly indebted to our project advisers, Michael Byram and Duarte Silva, for their valuable input, their critical thoughts and for their continuous support throughout this project.

We also valued greatly the co-operative spirit and the constructive criticism of all our workshop participants.

Our sincere thanks to our research fellow Anne-Sofia Holmberg for her much appreciated help in preparation for and during the workshop, and in particular for her valuable contributions to our quantitative study.

The ECML ICOPROMO project was complementary to and benefited from the Leonardo da Vinci ICOPROMO project that was funded by the EU's Leonardo da Vinci programme. The co-ordinator of the project was Manuela Guilherme, Centro de Estudos Sociais, Universidade de Coimbra.

Table of contents

Preface

Mike Byram and Duarte Silva

The field of intercultural studies, education and training has exploded in recent years. The reasons are obvious enough as globalisation and internationalisation have become familiar phenomena, having an impact in myriad ways on all of us. Whether it is a phone call from a call-centre in another continent, a pair of shoes bought in one country which have travelled half way or more around the world, daily contact with people of visibly different origins – wearing different clothing, having different habits, eating different food, identifying with different religions – all of these things have appeared in less than a generation.

For many people the experience is changing within their own environment. For others change comes through their move to another country as migrants, refugees or asylum seekers. For others again, it is a professional experience, and flying to another country once a week or travelling to another continent for a stay of several months is simply expected of them as "just part of the job".

Yet we know that this kind of professional mobility is not as simple as it appears. There are major demands on someone who has to metaphorically and literally "find their way" in a new cultural environment, and they may equally become "lost" both literally and metaphorically. As a consequence, a practical interest has arisen in cross-cultural training for those who are professionally mobile, which has flourished in recent decades. Much of this is based on common-sense and intuition but there has also been a realisation that there is a need for sound theoretical understanding. Otherwise it is possible to do more harm than good, to reinforce prejudice and overgeneralisation, for example, to advocate stereotypical response to new experience.

What the ICOPROMO project offers is a thorough theoretical grounding and a large number of training activities which reflect a rich understanding of a complex phenomenon. The model identifies the key elements and their relationships. It is dynamic, demonstrating the role of the different elements in the change which follows from reaction to the challenge of what the team call "the new world order". It is this dynamic character which is its great merit. It allows those involved, whether as the people who are mobile or those who are preparing them to become mobile, to conceptualise the experience and thus feel more comfortable with it.

A model does not, however, guarantee a "safe landing" any more than the preparatory activities one might undertake, but it helps us to understand what is happening. In any case, a "safe landing" is not always the best thing. The challenge of the new, the culture shock it brings, is no more than an opportunity to learn, to become different, to "unlearn", in short to gain the new perspective that is part of any education. It is no more than that but it undoubtedly can be a particularly forceful, rich, demanding and sometimes destructive experience, like all educational experiences.

Because of the potential negative effects as well as the enrichment mobility can bring, people need preparation, need guidance, need time for reflection and the intellectual tools of analysis. This is what the ICOPROMO project offers in its model and activities, and it does so on the basis of a prior analysis of the needs of the professionally mobile people who are its primary audience.

There is no doubt, however, that the work of the group has wider significance and that their model and activities will be relevant to others in the field, whether trainers, researchers or other mobile groups. We have therefore been very happy to be involved in the project, to offer a small contribution and to see the project mature into a substantial and important product which is represented in these pages and in the CD-Rom which accompanies them.

We should not forget, either, the difficulties of working on such projects, which to some degree mirror the demands made on the mobile professionals for which the team was working. They too have had to fly, to work in intensive seminars, to meet deadlines, to write in another language, to administer finances, to leave their families behind during their weekends and free time, to keep the momentum on this project going whilst dealing with other projects, responsibilities in their own universities and so on. This is the internationalised, globalised world which impacts as much on academic workers as on other professionals.

It has been a pleasure to be involved, to see the team themselves evolve, as well as the product they present here. It can now fly free and will, we are sure, be admired by all who encounter it.

Introduction: How to use this publication

Evelyne Glaser

This publication combines a printed document and a CD-Rom. In the printed document the reader will find essential information on the ICOPROMO project and on the theoretical model developed within its framework. This section is mainly intended as background reading to enhance the understanding of the materials designed for the development of intercultural competence. The project team feels that all those who are interested in the enhancement of intercultural competence using our training activities will find it valuable to gain a deeper insight into the theoretical concepts underlying these materials.

In addition to the texts that also appear in printed form, the CD-Rom features a set of 18 training activities designed to develop the intercultural competence of a multicultural workforce, especially of people working in multicultural teams. Every activity included in this collection aims at fostering some particular skills that are briefly defined in the rationale of each activity. A more detailed description can be found in the text on our model. Depending on the precise needs and interests of a specific target group, the facilitators will be able to choose those activities they deem most suitable. In other words, there is no strict sequence that has to be observed in using our materials. Below, the reader will find a table that provides an overview of the activities included and the respective competences they aim to develop.

The CD-Rom also contains a fairly detailed analysis of a qualitative study on multicultural teams carried out in the four countries represented by the original project team (Austria, Germany, Portugal and Spain). The results from this study were used to define the main elements of our model. Finally, the reader will find an analysis of a survey on the topics of languages and cross-cultural training in 30 international businesses and organisations.

Table of activities for the enhancement of intercultural competence

Intercultural competence	Name of activity	Time required
Awareness of the self and the other	What I am/ have/should	45 minutes
	Who's talking funny?	40 minutes
	A name, a self	40-55 minutes
	Preferences	45 minutes
Communicating across cultures	Rich points	55-70 minutes
	Language and reality	40-50 minutes
	It's a puzzling world	70 minutes
	Tu es anglaise?	30 minutes
	Non-verbal communication and body language	50 minutes
Acquiring cultural knowledge	All eyes and ears	120 minutes (site visit) 45 minutes
Sense-making	Journey to the unconscious	40-50 minutes
	I speak English, I am literate	50 minutes
Perspective-taking	Not like you	120 minutes
	Perspective taking	60 minutes
Relationship-building	Where do I belong?	20-30 minutes
	"Languaging" through e-mail	90 minutes
Assuming social responsibility	The common and the divergent	90 minutes
	Just words, not bullets	120 minutes

The ICOPROMO project

Evelyne Glaser

1.   Rationale for the ICOPROMO project

Professional contacts are increasingly taking place across cultural and linguistic boundaries. However, not everyone who is called upon to work with people from other cultures in the professional world has been appropriately prepared to meet the challenges involved in what we define as "intercultural interactions". In fact, very few educational institutions in the field of the social sciences have successfully managed to combine the development of intercultural competencies with the language education in their programmes. Hence, their graduates often find it hard to cope with cultural differences, particularly when working in multicultural teams, and they often lack the necessary cultural knowledge or mindfulness.

The team members of this project therefore feel that the Intercultural competence for professional mobility (ICOPROMO) project can make a useful contribution towards greater social cohesion across cultures. In addition, the ICOPROMO project intends to foster personal fulfilment, active citizenship, and social and professional inclusion by facilitating managers' and workers' mobility. It intends to stimulate ongoing discussions about the value and necessity of language/culture education for professional purposes.

The objective of the ICOPROMO project was firstly to produce a comprehensive and integrated model that can serve as a theoretical underpinning for educators and learners in the field of language and culture. At the same time, this model aims to contribute towards a visualisation of the ongoing and cyclical developmental process that is characteristic of intercultural competence. As with the acquisition of languages, one never attains complete mastery in this field. Secondly, the project team developed a set of activities to be used in training situations with the designated target groups. Each activity addresses one particular aspect of the development of intercultural competence as defined by the project team in the ICOPROMO model.

The materials developed in this project are primarily targeted at educators and facilitators working with:

- undergraduate and graduate students (with a background in social sciences), who are preparing for their professional careers;

- managers and employees, with an academic background in the social sciences, who are either preparing to work in different cultural surroundings or who need to develop language and cultural awareness to cope with the intercultural workplace.

However, all those who are preparing adults from other areas for interaction processes with members of different cultures may also find the activities and the underlying theory useful.

The project focuses on group-oriented (teamwork), rather than on individually oriented, intercultural communication and interaction competencies. It identifies and recognises non-formal learning settings (namely, cross-cultural experience) and uses them as the basis for formal education and further improvement of existing language and culture skills. It aims to promote lifelong and reflective learning and tries to integrate language and culture awareness within domain-specific knowledge. With its double focus on language learning and the development of intercultural competences, the ICOPROMO project finds itself aligned with the aims propagated by the Council of Europe in its European Language Portfolio and the Language Passport. The activities targeted to learners at B2 and C1 level as defined by the Common European Framework of Reference for Languages intend to enhance both language and culture learning.

The proposed activities will help learners to become aware of the deep-rooted assumptions, ideas and emotions pertaining to their own as well as the target culture(s). The training participants will come to realise how these influence their (selective) perceptions of the other. Attributions and categorisations that frequently guide cross-cultural communicative behaviour will be brought to the fore, questioned and hopefully modified/discarded. The aim of these activities is to provide the members of multicultural teams with the necessary background to work comfortably and efficiently with representatives from other cultures in ways that honour the backgrounds and identities of all parties involved.

2.   Stages of the ICOPROMO project

Throughout the three-year project, the ICOPROMO project team consisting of Evelyne Glaser (Austria), Manuela Guilherme (Portugal), María del Carmen Méndez García (Spain) and Terry Mughan (UK) (who replaced Susanne Weber, Germany, in 2005) was very actively supported by their advisers, Michael Byram (Durham University) and Duarte Silva (Stanford University).

During the initial stage of the ICOPROMO project, the team conducted a thorough search for existing literature on intercultural competence, intercultural communication and multicultural teams, the aim of which was to provide the necessary theoretical background and framework. We specifically looked at theories on cross-cultural communication (for example, Agar, 1994a, 1994b; Bennett, 1998; Brislin and Yoshida, 1994; Byram et al., 2001, 2003; Kramsch, 1993, 2003; Seelye, 1995, 1996; Ting-Toomey, 1999; Ting-Toomey and Oetzel, 2001) and tried to relate them to management theories on culture (for example, Adler, 1997; Hofstede, 1980, 1991; Hall, 1976; Trompenaars, 1994; Hampden-Turner and Trompenaars, 2000). We also took note of and built on previous projects on related topics carried out under the auspices of the ECML, such as *Mirrors and Windows: An Intercultural Communication Textbook* (Huber-Kriegler, Lázár and Strange, 2003), *ODYSSEUS: Second Language at the Workplace* (Grünhage-Monetti, Halewijn and Holland, 2003) or *Social Identity and the European Dimension: Intercultural Competence Through Foreign Language Learning* (Byram and Tost Planet (eds.), 2000) to ensure that the ICOPROMO project would not repeat any existing work.

Subsequently, a comprehensive qualitative research study was carried out in Austria, Germany, Portugal and Spain among managers and employees with extensive experience in multicultural teams. From this research we were able to derive the existing needs and requirements that our training activities would have to cater for. At a later stage we also carried out a quantitative study among European companies on questions related to in-company language and culture training. More details on these studies can be found in the chapters that follow.

The third stage involved the development of a tentative theoretical model for the development of intercultural competence for professional mobility. Simultaneously, we also designed a number of training activities to be used in multicultural and/or monocultural teams. Their aim is to raise awareness of one's own and the other's culture and to enhance communication skills, as well as the abilities of sense-making, perspective-taking and relationship-building. Finally, trainees should also be made aware of their social responsibility in a multicultural working environment and to manage diversity effectively. In brief, they should be led to question their own social behaviour patterns and habits, and to change them in such a way that they can move successfully between cultures.

In an ECML workshop in October 2005, 23 participants from 22 European countries came to Graz and co-operated actively with the ICOPROMO team in testing and improving the activities. The team is greatly indebted to AVL List GmbH and GIBS (Graz International Bilingual School) for hosting a group of workshop participants and for allowing them to carry out an ethnographic activity for the ICOPROMO project on their premises. This enabled the project team and the workshop participants to contextualise today's corporate and organisational needs and realities as a backdrop to reviewing and testing the ICOPROMO training activities.

The final stages of the project focused on the revision of our earlier model and on the preparation of the project publication. Even though the ICOPROMO team members make no claim for the project's completeness and perfection, they hope that their work will enable the defined target groups to extend their range of skilled intercultural behaviours and to open them up to the rich experience of moving successfully between cultures.

ICOPROMO: A transformational model

Evelyne Glaser, Manuela Guilherme, María del Carmen Méndez García, Terry Mughan

1. Introduction

The ICOPROMO model[1] is transformational in that it articulates the journey the individual undergoes when becoming aware of intercultural challenges as a result of his/her mobility or that of others with whom he/she must communicate effectively. It then describes how and what that individual must learn in order to communicate more effectively, the impact of that learning on his/her attitudes, behaviour and communicative performance and the on-going experience of encountering new challenges and learning new knowledge and techniques to meet them.

This journey begins on the left-hand side for most of us when some aspect of the political or economic environment exposes us to cultural difference. *The new world order*[2] and its impact on *the individual* cause him/her to be removed (physically and/or psychologically) from the home environment (or "comfort zone") and to encounter cultural difference. At that point both the traveller and the environment are faced with *challenges* of a cultural and linguistic nature which must be met in order for material, physical and emotional needs to be satisfied. All human beings have their own personal *dispositions* to this kind of challenge. Some feel totally disorientated by a foreign environment and others appear to be able to adapt to it quickly. Learning needs are therefore highly personal and everybody needs different kinds and degrees of support in order *to cope with* the situation. Coping here can be seen as the process by which the individual feels able to reliably process data and respond appropriately in order to achieve their objectives.

At an educational level, those needs can be expressed as *"competences"* the traveller needs to possess. Through reviews of relevant literature and empirical work, the ICOPROMO project has identified a series of these that are listed in the large central box. These competences stretch from the process of using language effectively to the challenge of understanding one's role and responsibilities to the new environment as a citizen of it. They entail both cognitive and behavioural (skills) development which can be achieved through study and training. They are learned through participation in the

---

1 When viewed in colour the model has the appearance of horizontal traffic lights. On the left side, where the learner encounters cultural difference and starts his/her journey, the box is red. The learning phases in the central boxes are shades of amber and when the individual has completed these and is able to move forward on the right, the box is green.

2 For a fuller explanation of the terms highlighted in bold and italics, turn to Section 2

range of activities that accompany this text and can be found on the CD-Rom. Most are best carried out in groups and led by a capable trainer/facilitator.

These groups, rather like many professional organisations and teams, will themselves be composed of people of differing cultural and linguistic backgrounds. Language, both verbal and non-verbal, is the prime means by which communication takes place. Thus, the very thing about which the traveller is learning (intercultural competence) is the means by which he/she is receiving and processing that knowledge (medium). How well he/she learns is to some extent determined by the degree of competence in the language and knowledge of the culture. *Interlanguage/interculture* in the model expresses this interdependence between the intercultural competence and the medium and how mindful we need to be of the effect they have on each other and the overall process of learning.

The development of intercultural competence therefore involves the learning of certain knowledge and values and the re-evaluation and discarding of existing ones which may conflict with them. Alongside *learning, unlearning* therefore takes place and this is an iterative process.

In completing these activities, the traveller will re-evaluate many of the attitudes which have been accumulated as a monocultural entity, for example, the tendency when faced with a critical incident immediately to attribute stereotypes to all members of a foreign culture without qualification or reflection. The process of *attitudinal change* as he/she learns to respond differently by instead pausing and asking himself/herself whether there may be another explanation leading to *behavioural change* as he/she learns to inquire rather than opinionate. Cumulatively, therefore, as the traveller adapts to challenges of this type, he/she becomes mobile with an intercultural mindset not a monocultural one. This is, however, not a finite point as he/she constantly finds himself/herself exposed to new incidents, stimuli and challenges which need more information, learning and reflection to inform an appropriate response. This is particularly the case in professional contexts where the mix of nationalities and locations is increasingly rich. Teams of people face business challenges which expose the traveller to organisational pressures as well as technical and personal challenges and the amount of information and relationships to be managed is constantly growing. This causes him/her to review, re-visit and refer to new sources of learning to become more *interculturally mobile* and competent.

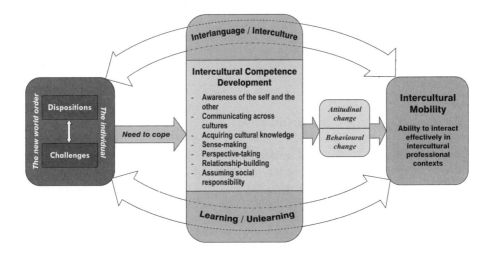

*Figure 1. ICOPROMO – The development of intercultural competence:
a transformational model*

2. The new world order and the individual

2.1 External factors

The need for intercultural competence on the part of professionals and the provision of training programmes for this purpose has been long established in the diplomatic and military spheres where medium/long-term overseas placements are commonplace. Since the Second World War a similar need began to emerge in large multinational companies, mainly American, which chose to staff their international subsidiaries with American executives. These expatriate executives, often accompanied by their spouses and children, would be supported in their preparation for and acclimatisation to their new home by means of training, advice and help in domestic as well as management matters. The expatriation model was largely responsible for the emergence and growth of the intercultural training industry, even though it was based on a simple business model and a limited marketplace. In recent years, a much larger and more diverse demand for intercultural competence has begun to emerge, driven by economic, political and social change on a global scale.

Since the fall of the Berlin Wall in 1989 and the ensuing collapse of the Communist Bloc, the fundamental nature of world trade has changed and the amount of goods and labour crossing national borders has increased dramatically. Simultaneously, rapid advances in information and satellite technology have made the world smaller and brought foreign subsidiaries closer to each other and to headquarters. Air travel has been deregulated and hence become cheaper, and human mobility across borders for business and tourism has increased significantly. On a political level this mobility takes many forms; on the one hand, as a new personal freedom because of professional opportunities and new trade agreements (EU, NAFTA, APEC) and, on the other, as enforced migration because of conflicts such as those in Bosnia and Kosovo.

2.2   Growth in world trade and investment

Between 1980 and 2000 world exports of goods have almost doubled, reaching US$7 000 billion in 1999 and accounting for almost 22% of world domestic product. Over the same time period, flows of world foreign direct investment have quadrupled, reaching around US$500 billion in 1999 (Wall and Rees, 2001). Of course all these developments took place within an environment of increasing competitiveness and the aggregate figures disguise large differentials at regional and national levels. For example, labour costs even within the European Union are extremely variable, up to three times higher in Belgium than in Portugal in 1997 (Wall and Rees, 2001).

Much of this growth has been facilitated by the liberalisation of most of the world's economies, guided by institutions such as the General Agreement on Tariffs and Trade (GATT) and the World Trade Organization. As countries have signed up to agreements to open up their domestic markets to international competition, they have effectively joined an international market in labour whereby they both import and export human resources more easily. The number of cross-border mergers and acquisitions grew fourfold between 1990-99 (Kang, 2001). This activity impacts directly on the shape and culture of the organisations affected, increasing mobility, cross-border communications and stress for many of the individuals involved.

2.3   Communications – Air travel and information technology

One of the earlier consequences of the liberalisation of markets was the privatisation of many branches of the airline industry. Within a relatively short period in the late 1980s, nationalised companies such as British Airways and Air France were exposed to new sources of competition for routes and increasing pressure on costs and prices. The arrival of the "budget" airlines such as Ryanair and EasyJet made air travel cheaper and easier. Between 1980 and 1999 the number of international tourists more than doubled from 260 million to 600 million travellers a year (Wall and Rees, 2004).

Rapid progress in information technology and its uses, such as the Internet and videoconferencing have also created means by which individuals and companies can access and manage information in new ways. Larger companies have intranets at their disposal to store and update product, financial and market information and these can be accessed from anywhere in the world. Project teams can communicate daily, face-to-face, on the Web and to do this effectively new skills and protocols are needed to

18

ensure good communication. These employees have to take differences of time, language and culture into account if they are to be effective in e-mails and videoconferences.

2.4   The impact on multinational companies and their organisational structure

A much-discussed consequence of these increased trade flows and communication channels is their impact on companies, how they structure themselves and attempt to respond to market change. Bartlett and Ghoshal (1998) tracked the development of the international corporation and propose that the evolution from the multi-domestic model, through the international and global models to the currently dominant transnational model reflect the historical shifts in global economy and the need of the large corporation to restructure internally to respond to external changes in the marketplace. This evolution is essentially one of a shift from a hierarchical, centralised structure based on the primacy of the nation-state based headquarters to a matrix whereby all global units of the organisation leverage market advantage, innovation and economies of scale in a multidirectional set of relationships. This gives rise to a flexible working regime where an individual employee might report to a line manager in the same building as him/herself for functional purposes and also to a manager in a far-off country for the purposes of product development or project management. This form of corporate operations necessitates the creation of virtual teams who communicate and manage projects electronically across great distances without necessarily ever meeting up.

The challenge for smaller companies is to institute similar forms of communication with fewer resources. Those which succeed in positioning themselves in a supply-chain driven by a large company are sometimes able to partner and network using the larger firm's resources. Individuals working for any company that is active in international markets are nowadays faced with a bewildering range of challenges and channels to market that have to be constantly mastered and updated.

2.5   Education and exchange programmes

Students constitute an important part of the mobile global population. There are for example more than 50 000 Chinese students studying in the United Kingdom. Some managers and entrepreneurs are given a flying start in their professional careers by the opportunity to spend part of their undergraduate studies in a foreign university. The ever-increasing use of English in academic and professional circles is creating opportunities to live and study abroad and thereby increase their employability and attractiveness to employers. The European Commission's ERASMUS programme funds the university to develop links and accreditation and the student to travel to the foreign university.

Graduate employers across the world frequently cite "international experience" or "a cosmopolitan mindset" as one of the leading criteria for selection of graduates for training programmes. The Bologna Declaration (1999) foresees continuing convergence among national educational programmes and increasing mobility of products and resources, though many students embark on their programmes with very little intercultural preparation.

2.6   Migration due to EU enlargement and political unrest

In the European Union around 20 million people are migrants (Euractiv, 2006). Migration takes many different forms, political or economic, temporary or permanent, social or professional. The events in Bosnia and Kosovo in the 1990s and the expansion of the European Union in 2005 created waves of migrants from low-wage countries wishing to seek work in Europe's more advanced economies. Not only do these workers contribute labour, they also become part of the host community, contributing to its culture and diversity and drawing on its social, educational and health resources. This generates cultural and linguistic interaction which may be a source of richness but also of inefficiency if not actively managed. Whether it be a matter of immigrants working as doctors, nurses, IT specialists or labourers, we now live in an era where cultural difference comes to us at home and poses challenges that we have to address on several levels; citizenship and social cohesion, equality of opportunity and workplace relations and efficiency.

2.7   Personal factors

The events outlined in the previous sections can be interpreted both positively and negatively. They have generated opportunities and threats to communities, organisations and, most importantly, individuals. The person entering another culture, whether as a professional or as a migrant, can be seen either as an intruder or a saviour, or both. He/she needs to be able to understand the dynamics of mobility and develop the appropriate skills to ensure they can both satisfy their own requirements and goals and be seen to contribute to the community. To achieve this they have to first of all confront their own predispositions and ready themselves to embrace difference. This is not always easy, particularly when they are separated from family and friends, unable to use language freely and confidently, and struggling to satisfy some basic material and psychological needs.

What we know about culture shock (Marx, 2001) is largely derived from studies of the expatriation model outlined in the introduction to this chapter. That means it is based on the corporate executive and his family travelling within a relatively well-resourced context. In spite of this, estimates of the number of failed assignments, whilst hard to get right, generally are quite high. Intercultural communication theories, which include concepts such as tolerance of ambiguity, active listening and mindfulness, may only partly explain the mentality and behaviour of the international student, the migrant worker or the virtual team. Can we transpose the expatriation model onto these new communities or do we need new research? Probably the latter but in the meantime it is probably safe to assume that the fears and insecurities of intercultural travellers are real and need to be addressed on a social, educational and organisational level.

2.8   Conclusion

Globalisation, however we choose to define it, entails greater degrees of human mobility on all levels than was the case up until the 1980s. People from a larger number of countries, of varying levels of education and of different professional backgrounds now find themselves in critical intercultural contact, at home or abroad, in person or electronically, with members of other cultures. Increased trade, migration and corporate integration equals greater occurrence of intercultural professional contact and a corresponding demand for communication skills. The ICOPROMO project was designed to contribute to meeting this demand.

3.   Dispositions and behavioural change

3.1   Introduction

As with all types of learning, trainees can benefit differentially from intercultural training depending on the one hand on factors external to the learning context (as previously discussed) and on the other on their individual dispositions or motivations (namely, their abilities, motives, expectations, willingness) (Caligiuri, 2006). This means that any given intercultural training activity will not necessarily achieve the same results with everybody. The ICOPROMO model suggests that in order for the individual to develop intercultural competence it is necessary to trigger behavioural and attitudinal change. The likelihood or unlikelihood of this change happening is dependent on personality factors. In order to reach some understanding on how these personality factors (dispositions) impact attitudes and behaviour, it is necessary to look at some basic theories of psychology.

3.2   Psychological theories on dispositions

3.2.1   Field theory

Field Theory, developed by Kurt Lewin (1935), emphasised that a person's behaviour (B) can best be understood by studying the interaction between his/her personality (P) and environmental pressures (E):

$$B_P = f(P, E)$$

This means that one's behaviour is related to both one's personal characteristics (dispositions) and to the social situation in which one finds oneself. Hence, dispositions, in order to be activated, require also external/environmental factors. Psychology traditionally differentiates between motivational and cognitive dimensions when referring to a person's intrinsic dispositions. The complexity of the motivational and cognitive dimensions involved here is illustrated in Figure 2.

3.2.2 Drive factors

As Figure 2 shows, a basic distinction must be made between drive factors and abilities. The drive factors are the core of motivational theories, while the abilities find their home in learning theories. In practice, both work as an integrative system. The bases of drive factors are motives. Motives have two dimensions and are anchored in the subconscious realm of the human being. They consist of a driving force and are also directly connected with a special content. So, if we speak of a "power motive", the content consists of the disposition to influence other people and the driving force is the attempt to display a behaviour that will achieve this goal. Whether this goal is actually achieved or not depends on external factors, namely on the specific nature of the interaction with other parties and specifically on the willingness of others to follow an individual who assumes power.

The scope of the content of motives is manifold. Especially, three areas captured the interest of psychologists: McClelland (1961) focused mainly on achievement, power and affiliation motives. Berlyne (1950) concentrated his research primarily on the curiosity drive which itself consists of many forms ranging from sheer nosiness and the wish to explain trivial things to the desire to reach an understanding of nature and finally of the essence of human existence.

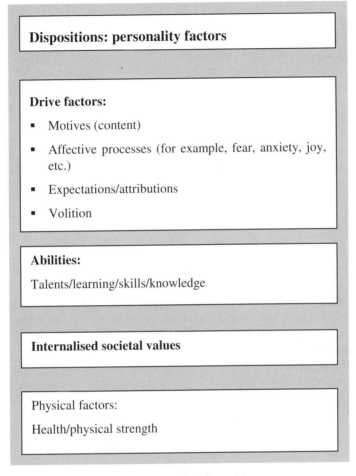

Figure 2. Model of dispositions

Weick (1996) underpinned such a curiosity need with his theory of sense-making. Sense-making is an attempt to reduce multiple meanings (equivocality) and handle complex information used by people in an organisation. In his constructivist approach, behaviour comes first, is observed by the person who then tries to explain the reasons for this behaviour and gives it (invents) thereby a sense.

The cognitive dissonance theory by Festinger (1957) adds to the sense-making process the concept that human beings actively try to create a consonant picture of their subjective world. Thus, according to cognitive dissonance theory, individuals tend to seek consistency among their cognitions (that is, beliefs, opinions). When there is an inconsistency between attitudes or behaviours (dissonance), something must change to eliminate the dissonance. In the case of a discrepancy between attitudes and behaviour, it is most likely that the attitude will change to accommodate the behaviour.

Within the framework of this theory, the importance of commitment/volition was rediscovered, a concept that was originally very important in the *Willenspsychologie* in the early 1900s in the German psychological literature. This idea is also connected to Freud's concept of the ego and the socially determined superego. The term "commitment" actually underlines the driving force of decision making which is based on the subjective perception that the person has a choice between alternative ways of action. For example, if a person after a thorough search has made a decision to buy a special brand of car, the person changes from a neutral researcher to a "committed" driver of this car and gives this vehicle a much higher value than before the decision. Along the same lines, it is very important for students to have a choice in the selection of the languages they want to study, as the conscious decision in favour of a certain language is a very important factor for motivation and commitment to make progress and eventually achieve mastery.

The reference to Sigmund Freud underlines another aspect of personality factors, namely the phenomenon of conflict. Despite all tendencies to avoid cognitive dissonance, the human being has to struggle not only with external conflicts but also with inner disparities. Thus, a child may want to pet a dog but is afraid at the same time that the dog may bite him. Along these lines, Lewin (1935) differentiates between three kinds of conflicts: (a) avoidance-approach conflicts as described in the above example, (b) avoidance-avoidance conflicts, for example to pursue the language-learner analogy, the person has to choose between a written and an oral examination in the language he/she is studying and likes neither of them, or (c) an approach-approach conflict, in which the person cannot decide between two positive alternatives which have an equal appeal to him/her, like travelling to different countries and staying at home. In his field theory, Lewin shows how such situations can find a resolution with or without the help of other persons.

A second factor was added in the development of motivational theories by including cognitive factors in the form of expectations. These expectations are based on the experiences in the learning process of the person. A complex concept is, for example, the theory of self-efficacy by Bandura (1994). In this concept the behavioural disposition depends on different factors which bring the person to the conviction that he/she will be successful in mastering a task, and, for example, will be able to learn a language. Conversely, the individual has had a previous negative experience that earlier aspirations in this area were always unsuccessful. Therefore his/her self-efficacy will be low with regard to language acquisition. So, for a behavioural tendency it is not only important to have a motive for something but also the expectation that the content of this motive can be achieved. As Bandura (1986) says, "Self-efficacy is the belief in one's capabilities to organise and execute the sources of action required to manage prospective situations." Hence, if an individual holds high expectations that he/she can become culturally competent through training, the chances are higher that this can actually be achieved.

Besides motives and expectations, emotions/affections accompany the motivational process. They are also anchored in the subconscious of a human being. Such emotions/affections may act as a leitmotif of the character of a person, for example, they are responsible for the fact that a person is generally fearful and full of angst, or might be melancholic, or very cheerful and outgoing. These are long-lasting characteristics that can occasionally be interrupted by shorter eruptions of emotions like joy or anger.

3.2.3 Abilities/societal values/physical factors

Another dimension of the inner structure of a personality consists of **values**. They are internalised by the socialisation process in dependence and interaction with the micro or macro social environment. Besides all these driving forces, the human being is equipped with abilities, talents and the acquired knowledge through learning processes. The development of knowledge can be based on trial and error or on vicarious (imitative) behaviour.

All these psychological dimensions are embedded in the physical characteristics of a person. Modern learning theories have provided very interesting results on the functioning of the brain and are very helpful for the design of a learning process.

3.3   Moderators and mediators of behavioural change

This inner repertoire of the human being should be diagnosed when we attempt to influence behaviour through intervention, which is in our case when we try to enhance intercultural competence through training. In order to be successful, we should strive to achieve a fit between a person's dispositions and our training instruments. This means that the training methods have to be adapted to an individual. Therefore, it is very important to consider which factors of the personality are stable and which ones show enough elasticity and thus may result in a propensity to change. When looking at motivational dispositions, the dominating motive structure is a very stable factor. Consequently, it will be easier to adjust the cognitive factors and the environmental conditions for learning. Obviously, training can be much more effective if a person shows signs of open-mindedness and if he/she is equipped with a high degree of curiosity and achievement orientation. In contrast, a person who shows a dominating failure-avoidance motive and a low self-efficacy in his/her learning history, especially in the area of languages and the understanding of cultural differences will hardly be affected by an intercultural training course. This is very important for a trainer to know, because the motivational dispositions of a trainee may be structured in such a way that it may be difficult to effect any changes in behaviour or attitudes.

Locke and Latham (1990) integrate most of the aforementioned motivational and cognitive variables into a model of work behaviour which they call the "high performance cycle". This cycle starts with high goals or meaningful, growth-facilitating tasks or a series of tasks. These tasks are self-selected or provided by other persons (for example, supervisors, colleagues, teachers, family members). The performance as the fulfilment of the tasks depends on the complicated interaction between "moderators" and "mediators". In this model, the abilities, commitments (volition), expectations and the self-efficacy of the person are considered as the moderators, whereas the task complexity is viewed as the environmental factor. Among the mediators, Locke and Latham highlight two factors which are rarely included in motivational theories but seem to have an important influence on a "high performance" learning process, namely efforts and persistence as internal personality factors. Their importance has recently been confirmed by anatomical studies of the brain. Gusnard et al. (2003) found that students who scored highest in persistence had the highest activity in the limbic region, the area of the brain related to emotions and habits. The "high performance cycle" continues when the performance is reinforced with "rewards" and with the experience of satisfaction or dissatisfaction. The level of satisfaction is not seen "as the start" of the performance process or as accompanying the performance process in this model, but is placed "at the end" of the cycle. However, it determines the consequences of efforts made. With the degree of satisfaction the individual's willingness to accept future challenges increases.

3.4 Conclusion

To conclude this short overview of personality factors and the psychological structure of a person, we can sum up the general consequences as follows:

There is a clear interdependence between the current emotional state of a person and his/her current situation/environment in the way they influence human behaviour. In other words, if there is no fit (agreement) between a person's dispositions and the environment, there will be only limited behavioural change. Consequently, if intercultural competence training in a professional context (as an intervention) is to result in behavioural or even attitudinal change, the environment (that is, the training itself or the professional situation) must be attractive for the individual. The facilitators should therefore ensure that the learning environment is propitious and that the learners can clearly recognise the advantages they can gain for their private and professional lives by taking part in such training.

4. Challenges

The introduction of the concept of "challenge" in an intercultural competence model entails the recognition of the difficulties which emerge from intercultural encounters and even more so from the development of intercultural relationships, both at a professional and a personal level. However, it also entails an acknowledgement of the multiple and enriching possibilities that such encounters and relationships may provide.

4.1 Awareness

The very first challenge that one faces in an intercultural encounter is the awareness that one's own perspective is rooted and therefore limited. Although recognising this may at first be paralysing or confusing, it opens up immense opportunities for expanding one's horizon (Gadamer, 1970; Bhabha, 1994). This experience will thereby result in a redefinition and a new articulation of one's affiliations and of the earlier stable configuration of one's identity (Hall, 1996).

Foreign language/culture and intercultural learning are essential in processes like these, processes of engaging with different world visions, and are therefore crucial in raising awareness of one's horizon and, consequently, of its limits (Byram and Zarate, 1997; Giroux, 1992). The development of critical cultural awareness should be identified as a main goal for the development of intercultural competence and ultimately for intercultural active citizenship (Guilherme, 2002). The methods for raising intercultural awareness which have been used mainly in activities related to foreign language/culture education and in some professional development programmes are namely: ethnography (Roberts et al., 2001), authentic text hermeneutics (Kramsch, 1993); and focusing on metacognition (Earley and Ang, 2003).

4.2 Communication and interaction

Success in intercultural communication/interaction has been described as an interaction which is appropriate and/or effective (Smith, Paige and Steglitz, 1998; Guilherme, 2000; Ting-Toomey and Chung, 2005: 17-18). Success follows from meeting the requirements of the host culture or negotiating between one's linguistic/cultural background and the host culture one is engaging with both by taking from it and contributing to it. Both these alternative or complementary perspectives lie at the heart of intercultural communication and interaction and are common to different models which have been proposed for the development of intercultural competence and which aim either at assimilation into the host culture or at a pluralist integration. By definition, all models of intercultural communication/interaction exclude the option of rupture.

Several researchers have, however, described the process of engagement with other cultures not as an immediate event but as a progression made up of different stages. Bennett, for example, identifies two main stages at each end of the process of becoming interculturally competent, the "ethnocentric" and the "ethnorelative" (Bennett, 1993a). The first stage starts, according to the author, with the "denial" of differences, by emphasising what is common, or apparently common, in all human beings, and progresses into a "minimisation" stage where the individual admits some differences but tries to play them down. The "ethnorelative" stage starts with an "acceptance" stage and moves on to "integration". Bennett explains that intercultural individuals can reach different levels of the "integration" stage. They can try to articulate aspects of both cultures and, to some extent, construct a new identity which remains, nevertheless, rooted in the cultural, albeit multicultural, context. Or they can somehow live in a "constructive marginality" which enables them to become more independent from the cultural constraints of their immediate context (Bennett, 1993a).

Other authors, however, tend to adopt a more holistic approach to intercultural exchange and identify "cultural intelligence" as "a person's capacity to adapt effectively to new cultural contexts" (Early and Ang, 2003). In fact, effective intercultural communication and interaction is defined from different perspectives by different authors. It can entail: (a) an investigatory attitude, "understanding each others' styles and motives behind them, is a first move in overcoming intercultural misunderstanding" (Kim, 1998: 105); (b) a dialogical and relational attitude, where sheer communication and interaction, although with a purpose, is at stake (Byram, 1997); (c) a more or less respectful strategic attitude, which can imply a commitment to fulfil a task or to persuade, or even influence, the other (Byram, 1997); (d) a critical attitude, which implies a critical awareness of the motives and pressures experienced by all participants, of the power structures in both cultural contexts and of the interdependence and relations between them (Guilherme, 2002).

4.3   Power relations

Power relations are common to all cultures but their workings and the criteria on which they rely vary from society to society and from culture to culture. Therefore, "different types of power are effective in different cultural settings" (Pennington, 1989: 262). The challenge for intercultural communication and interaction in the multicultural workplace is to develop the attitudes and the skills which allow for relationship-building on democratic terms. According to Santos (2005: lxii), democracy "can be defined as the entire process through which unequal power relations are replaced by relations of shared authority". However, if authority is shared, the symbolic sources of influence in one's perception of the other, in connection with issues of gender, race, religion, etc., can still influence the dispositions that one brings to the intercultural encounter.

Foucault's notion of "capillary power" accounts for the proliferation of power games at the grass-roots level which is very helpful for understanding the negotiations which take place in professional teams or groups. Power can emerge from different sources of explicit and implicit authority, which can derive from formally appointed positions or from experience, knowledge, competence, social skills or even stronger from connections inside or outside the organisation. Each factor can have more or less impact depending on its weight within a specific culture. By developing intercultural competencies one becomes acquainted with different perspectives, aware of different criteria and familiar with processes of critical reflection and critical action that may, to some extent, prevent one from making absolute judgments and from unquestionably tracing a plan of action.

4.4   Ethics

Regulating decisions and behaviours are considered ethical when they conform to conventional beliefs, principles, values and moral standards which are particular to specific communities. The evaluation of the ethical justification of a decision or behaviour relies on judgments which are particular to specific communities and therefore "one of the critical ethical issues linked to cultural differences is the question of whose values and ethical standards take precedence" when there are conflicting ethical positions in a cross-cultural act of communication and interaction (Ferrell, Fraedrich and Ferrell, 2005: 219). This is frequently a challenge in the multicultural workplace, whether conflicting beliefs, principles, values and moral standards coexist within a society where a hierarchy is, explicitly or implicitly, established or where they have to cohabit temporarily in an even tug-of-war. Therefore, in such situations, intercultural competencies are challenged up to the point that a balance between the respect for one's dispositions, beliefs, principles, values and moral standards and one's attitudinal and behaviour change is reached and is equally acceptable for all participants.

4.5   Cultural dissonance

Diverse ethnic cultures coexist at different levels, namely local, regional, national and global. The latter is therefore not considered, in this case, universal but divided into European, American and Asian, and subdivided into north-south, east-west, etc. There are other variables that add or subtract to a broader or narrower notion of culture which can be identified with race, religion, gender, language, age, social and economic status, etc.

Therefore, "the workplace as a venue of communication simply changes the location of the interaction, not the predispositions and stereotypes that human beings bring to the situation" (Asante and Davis, 1989: 376). Communication and interaction in the workplace, although focused on a specific task and wrapped in the organisational culture, carry deep within a load of preconceptions and biases towards gender, race, religion, language, age and socioeconomic status, all of which have been part of one's socialisation in the family as well as in other informal and formal social contexts. Furthermore, even where there is a similarity in ethnic background, race, gender, language standards, age, and social and economic status, this does not guarantee effective communication. Nor, conversely, is it inevitable that the greater the cultural and/or geographic distance or the greater the difference in terms of the other categories mentioned above, the less effective their communication and interaction are.

Linguistic diversity and cultural dissonance are, therefore, a challenge in that they compel the individuals to be flexible and creative since they have to move, at the same time cautiously and daringly, in the fields of interlanguage and interculture. Furthermore, one is offered the opportunity to learn, unlearn and relearn new and old knowledge and, therefore, to challenge one's paradigms and re-read the world.

4.6   Sustainability

In a global world, it is equally important to find a common language and negotiate linguistic and cultural platforms for communicating and interacting as well as to provide for the expression of linguistic and cultural diversity. The concept of "lingua franca" – a language understood as being spoken freely by non-native speakers – relies on the idea that it can be constructed for that purpose or that it is adopted and deprived of its original cultural contents, but in none of the cases does it provide for authentic or meaningful communication. The use of a common language by culturally diverse non-native speakers implies, at least, linguistic and cultural translation and negotiation of meaning which can, at the same time, complicate and enrich communication and interaction.

The theory of the ecology of languages, arguing for the need for linguistic and cultural diversity and, as a result, for the balance of living conditions on earth, enhances the relevance of the development of intercultural competencies which enable individuals to make the most out of their linguistic and cultural exchanges while respecting the specificity of each language and culture (Skutnabb-Kangas, 2000). Similarly, the theory of the ecology of knowledge, which argues for the legitimacy of different knowledge patterns, as well as for the need for them for the survival of our planet, provides the framework for a paradigm of intercultural communication/interaction competence which is characterised by the actual recognition of cultural diversity (Santos, 2003). The acknowledgement of the importance of such ecologies, which do not dissociate humans from nature, is a fundamental element for understanding the dynamics of intercultural communication and interaction whereby individuals and groups communicate and interact democratically by developing a critical awareness of the self and the other, by valuing different languages, cultures and patterns of knowledge and by recognising different perspectives. This is indeed one of the main challenges which intercultural communication/interaction meets when it is based on reciprocal exchange, respectful dialogue and fair relationships, all leading to social justice.

5.   Intercultural competence development

5.1   Awareness of the self and the other

Awareness of the self and the other, getting to know oneself, reflecting upon one's culture-bound upbringing and standpoint and analysing in depth one's norms, values, beliefs and behaviours is probably the starting point towards accepting, understanding and enjoying otherness. The notion of identity comes to the foreground in this respect and its exploration seems to be a *sine qua non* for intercultural communication.

Awareness of the self and the other is linked to, at least, five sub-competences. Recognising similarities and differences, acknowledging that we all have things in common and aspects that make us different (not only as members of a particular culture but also as individuals) and exploring them becomes an enriching experience. From a personal perspective, assessing (personal inventory) and reflecting on one's own social construct turns out to be particularly revealing as it could be viewed as the necessity to embark on a journey inward with a critical mind, a guided tour throughout life with a view to evaluating one's viewpoints and social constructs. From the perspective of the others, finding out about the other lays the foundation for the intercultural encounter and it involves showing interest, curiosity and perseverance to know, find out about and truly understand the other.

From the perspective of the intercultural experience per se, exploring culture shock and reverse culture shock and considering stereotypes and generalisations prove to be essential. Dealing with culture shock and reverse culture-shock, particularly the latter as it is an unexpected phenomenon, is necessary on the part of the intercultural individual. Brislin and Pedersen (1976: 13) define culture shock as "the anxiety that happens when a person loses all the familiar cues to reality on which each of us depend". Culture shock seems to be experienced to some extent by people in intercultural contexts, predominantly when the individual enters a new culture. Instead of culture shock, which may seem hyperbolic, Szanston (1966: 44) prefers to talk about "cultural fatigue": "The physical and emotional exhaustion that almost invariably results from the infinite series of minute adjustments". However, the impact inherent in the intercultural contact does not end when the contact is over. Quite the opposite, contrary or reverse culture shock takes place once the individual returns to his/her original community and has to re-adjust to the old environment. This shock is termed by Brislin and Pedersen (1976: 16) "re-entry crisis" and tends to be a painful experience because it is a largely unexpected process. The intercultural individual needs to have the tools to cope with both culture shock and reverse culture shock. Together with culture shock, dealing with stereotypes and generalisations comes to the foreground in the intercultural experience. A stereotype 'is a category that singles out an individual as sharing assumed characteristics on the basis of his or her group membership" (Brown, 1994: 166). Stereotypes are harmful because they are said to derive from a grain of truth even though they are simply false because they disregard individual idiosyncrasy. Scollon and Scollon (1995: 155) relate stereotype with overgeneralisations and specify that "the difference, however, is that stereotyping carries with it an ideological position. Characteristics of the group are not only overgeneralized to apply to each member of the group, but they are also taken to have some exaggerated negative or positive value". Generalisations, on the other hand, making general assumptions about other groups because no more specific information is available, are necessary tools to help human beings get to grips with the enormous amount of information received every day. This is closely related to schema theory, which holds knowledge to be an intricate system of complex mental structures representing one's understanding of the world: "every act of comprehension involves one's knowledge of the world as well" (Anderson et al., 1983: 73). In sum, stereotypes are overgeneralisations with an inherent positive or negative load of added values.

5.2   Communicating across cultures

Communicating across cultures or intercultural communication is "communication on the basis of respect for individuals and equality of human rights as the democratic basis for social interaction" (Byram et al., 2002: 9). Communication across cultures involves acts of communication undertaken by individuals identified with groups exhibiting inter-group variation in shared social and cultural patterns (Damen, 1987).

Drawing a parallel between "intercultural communication" and "effective interaction", Guilherme (2000: 297-300) defines success in intercultural communication as "accomplishing a negotiation between people based on both culture-specific and culture-general features, that is on the whole respectful of and favourable to each". For Cohen (2004), "negotiation is an exercise in language and communication, an attempt to create shared understanding where previously there have been contested understandings. When negotiation takes place across languages and cultures the scope for misunderstanding increases. So much of negotiation involves arguments about words and concepts that it cannot be assumed that language is secondary". Accordingly, communication across cultures presents the problem that the selection of a lingua franca does not ensure that words and concepts are equally understood by all participants.

Three main sub-components have been identified as being an integral part of the competences that allow communicating across cultures: non-verbal communication, verbal communication and language awareness. Non-verbal communication occupies a relevant position in this paradigm. Communication does not exclusively depend on language; as Revell and Norman (1999: 91) indicate "communication is *more* non-verbal than verbal" (emphasis in the original). Non-verbal aspects may reinforce the message expressed verbally or, interestingly, they may contradict it. Even though most of them are not explicitly contemplated in the foreign language curriculum or syllabus, non-verbal aspects such as body language, eye contact, gestures, proxemics (interpersonal space), appearance, dressing style or haptics (bodily touching) seem to be highly significant in cross-cultural communication.

Verbal communication has no doubt been the central element of most foreign language programmes, with the first one out of the four main competences identified by Canale and Swain (1980: 7-11) extensively studied and practised:

■   grammatical competence (the "knowledge of lexical terms and rules of morphology, syntax, sentence-grammar, semantics, and phonology");

■   sociolinguistic competence ("made up of two sets of rules: sociocultural rules of use and rules of discourse");

32

- discourse competence (how to combine grammatical forms and meanings to achieve a unified spoken or written text in different genres);

- strategic competence (verbal and non-verbal communication strategies that may be called into action to compensate for breakdowns in communication due to performance variables or to insufficient competence).

Furthermore, paralinguistic features such as stress, rhythm and intonation play a fundamental role in verbal communication (for example, the tone used in a particular community such as the Spanish of Spain may seem aggressive in another Spanish-speaking community and may cause misunderstanding even though the linguistic code is shared).

Communication across cultures also rests on a third element, language awareness,[3] defined as the awareness of how speaking one or more languages or a particular language such as English is related to social/professional status. Different elements contribute to language awareness and, in particular, in the multicultural teamwork setting. First, the language selected in the intercultural encounter is worth exploring in depth. Multicultural team members should be aware of the fact that a specific language tends to predominate in the company or institution and that being a native or a proficient speaker of such a language may confer power on an individual. Second, it is equally relevant to heighten consciousness of the way in which one's native language may influence the manner in which we learn a foreign language and the degree of proficiency we attain in the latter.

Third, there exists a very interesting possibility of team members using an auxiliary code where their mother tongues are related (inter-comprehension) (Capucho, 2002; Doyé, 2005; Pencheva and Shopov, 2003; Rieder, 2002), in other words, when a certain language is selected as a lingua franca (for example, English), speakers of related and mutually intelligible languages (for example, Spanish and Portuguese) may benefit from using their own languages.

Fourth, there seems to be a need for mutual accommodation, with native speakers paying special attention not to use dialectical features – but a more standardised form of the language – and non-native speakers making an effort to make themselves understood in the lingua franca and feel confident to contribute their ideas and show persistence.

Fifth, it is paramount to heighten consciousness of tolerance of ambiguity (Gudykunst and Kim 1984; Anzaldua, 1987; Ronen, 1989; Stahl, 2001) given that, sometimes, the same message might be perceived or understood in different ways under the influence of different languages and cultures. When there is uncertainty, it is necessary to defer

---

3   This is based on an unpublished part of the manuscript "Language and Power: Raising Awareness of the Role of Language in Multicultural Teams" presented by Méndez García and Pérez Cañado at the IALIC Conference on Politics, Plurilingualism and Linguistic Identity, Dublin City University, 11-14 November 2004.

judgment and seek clarification, even though judgment may have to be deferred infinitely in certain circumstances.

Sixth, awareness of the existence of diverse communication styles (Gudykunst et al., 1996; Bennet, 1993; Saphiere et al., 2005) seems to be essential in intercultural exchanges. Certain national patterns seem to apply with regard to, for example, turn-taking, directness vs. indirectness, spoken vs. written preferences. Likewise, communication styles are based in situations: interrupting (when and how to do it), communicating among team members (German or English workers seem to prefer communicating via e-mail, whereas Spanish workers prefer speaking directly to each other), decision making in a formal (meeting) or informal way, direct vs. more indirect ways of speaking, etc. Furthermore, individuals within national cultures also have their own preferences and this individual variation becomes equally apparent in communication.

5.3   Acquisition of cultural knowledge

The third competence in a transformational model of intercultural competence for professional mobility turns out to be the acquisition of cultural knowledge, in the form of both culture general and culture specific knowledge (Brislin and Yoshida, 1994: 37-55). Culture general knowledge relates to the significance of possessing knowledge of the world. This is what Byram et al. (2002: 12) call "knowledge" or "*savoir*" of how human beings interact and perceive each other and how the way individuals perceive each other affects the way they interact. Apart from culture general knowledge, possessing some culture specific knowledge could prove beneficial in facilitating intercultural communication in a given society and/or with members of a particular community. Byram et al. (2002: 12) underline the need for individuals to be familiar with their own culture and that of the interlocutor.

5.4   Sense-making

The intercultural team member also has to develop the competence of sense-making, defined as the preparedness to deal with new information, uncertainty and ambiguity and to process these elements in a coherent way with pre-existing conceptual frameworks. As Dervin (1999: 740) points out, "Making sense assumes the actor as theorist of her world, with hunches, hypotheses, and generalisations about how things connect to things and how power flows". Olsson (2005: 2) relates sense-making with discourse analysis and social constructivist theory as sense-making ultimately depends on language: "Language is seen as the primary shaper of observations and interpretations of the world (see Dervin, 1991: 46-7; Dervin et al, 1992: 7). Information is about what people do with language and what language does to people (Talja, 1997: 71)."

Sense-making involves the capability to interpret documents, facts, incidents/events or any other emerging cultural artefact. This is very much related to what Byram et al. (2002: 13) call the "skills of interpreting and relating/*savoir comprendre*", defined as "the ability to interpret a document or event from other culture, to explain it and relate it to documents or events from one's own". But interpretation is not enough, sense-making also implies making meaning. The intercultural citizen has to make meaning of new or unexpected documents or events. In Byram et al.'s terms (2002: 13) these are the "skills of discovery and interaction/savoir *apprendre – faire*", the "ability to acquire new knowledge of a culture and cultural practices and the ability to operate knowledge, attitudes and skills under the constraints of real-time communication and interaction". Finally, sense-making entails identifying/perceiving and understanding prevalent values, beliefs and norms in a situation. These are not always apparent and failure to identify and understand them may well result in misunderstandings.

5.5 Perspective-taking

A fifth competence is perspective-taking, a highly demanding factor that requires the individual to look at reality from different viewpoints. It presupposes the capacity to see things from somebody else's position. This is a difficult task for human beings who are usually socialised in a particular community and therefore have deep-rooted beliefs, values and assumptions, most of them taken for granted and unconscious. Perspective-taking rests on qualities such as empathy, flexibility, decentring, open-mindedness and coping with ambiguity.

Empathy (for a discussion of empathy in multicultural teamwork see Chang and Tharenou, 2004; Cui and Awa, 1992; Wills and Barham, 1994) is the feeling or concern for others, which leads to some kind of personal and emotional identification. DiStefano and Maznevski (2000: 51-52) define empathy as almost getting into somebody's body and mind: "Empathy is getting inside another person's skin, thinking as the other person thinks and feeling what the other person feels". Byram (1989: 89), on the other hand, links empathy with tolerance, although he states that empathy is a more demanding process in that it is not only passive acceptance of otherness but it leads to real understanding and change of perspective. Both require the development of flexible attitudes and the capacity to decentre. Indeed, flexibility is closely related to showing adaptability and versatility in one's way of thinking and acting as opposed to being categorical and showing rigid patterns in communication with members of other cultures. The shift away from the "centre" implicit in the term "decentring" constitutes a challenge for intercultural citizens who, far from assuming that their cultural values, norms and beliefs are universal, are able to alter their standpoint and act accordingly when they become aware that their values, norms and beliefs are culturally determined. DiStefano and Maznevski (2000: 52) define decentring as "empathy in practice" or as "listening to others and responding to them" and state that it implies suspending judgment, fighting against the human tendency to judge the different as bad. Interestingly, for DiStefano and Maznevski (2000: 53) decentring is not the end, but it requires "recentring": "finding or developing shared ground upon which to build a new basis of interacting".

Intercultural contact on the basis of empathy, flexibility and decentring results in expanding one's horizon, as, undoubtedly, intercultural contact and experience provide the individual with excellent opportunities to revise their mental constructs, open up and enrich their perspectives. Lastly, perspective-taking involves a further quality, coping with ambiguity. It is understood as the competence that allows the interlocutor to deal with the uncertainty that arises when the context or the circumstances do not provide him/her with enough clues to make sense of the event successfully.

6. Interlanguage and interculture

6.1 Interlanguage

The term "interlanguage' was propounded by Selinker (1972) on the basis of Weinreich's (1953) concept of "interlingual". Selinker defined interlanguage as "the existence of a separate linguistic system based on the observable output which results from a learner's attempted production of a TL [target language] norm. This linguistic system we will call interlanguage" (Selinker, 1972: 214).

Interlanguage refers either to the individual's knowledge of the foreign language at a particular stage of development or at interlocked and different stages of their learning process. Even though the individual's interlanguage fluctuates in a continuum between the mother tongue and the target language, the interlanguage is independent of both, although inevitably linked to them. Indeed, an individual's interlanguage may contain features of their mother tongue, of the target language and further characteristics which belong to neither of them. In this sense, Selinker (1972) proposed "central processes" in interlanguage development such as language transfer (the use of rules learners extract from their first language), overgeneralisation (the generalisation of rules from the target language at the phonetic, grammatical, lexical and discourse levels to the extent that they would not be used by native speakers) and fossilisation (the possibility of terminating language learning in spite of frequent input and practice).

For Corder (1981), interlanguage is idiosyncratic in that, even though individuals with the same linguistic background may make similar errors, each person's interlanguage shows features that are unique. Corder (1981) defines interlanguage as having a system with a simple morphology, a relatively fixed word order, the use of simple personal pronouns, a reduced number of grammatical function words, scarce use of the copula and the absence of articles (Duran, 1994).

Interlanguages are dynamic in that as individuals' knowledge of the target language progresses and as their communicative competence increases, their interlanguage will gradually depart from the mother tongue to approach the target language. Therefore, interlanguages are "intermediate" systems of language development which would ideally coincide with the target language, although this native-like competence is very rarely achieved.

To sum up, teachers and learners constantly need to build upon the interlanguage that has already been acquired. Often the assumption is that they should build towards the native speaker as a model or an ideal. This is, however, in dispute today.

6.2   Interculture

The term "interculture" was developed by Kordes (1991: 300-301) by analogy with Selinker's notion of interlanguage. Interculture designates the transition stages between the native and the target culture learners have to go through in their approach to the target culture. Thus, interculture is defined as the individuals' degree of cultural competence, and this fluctuates between the native and the target culture and departs from the first culture as their familiarity with the target culture increases. Liddicoat (2005) argues that, like individuals' interlanguage, their interculture comprises characteristics of the first culture, features extracted from the target culture and further elements that belong to neither of them but that are peculiar to the learners in their way of hypothesising about and dealing with cultural phenomena.

However, in spite of the parallel in the process of target language and culture learning, Kordes (1991: 302) points out that it is more difficult to programme intercultural learning than language acquisition because the former is more complex than the latter.

Both, Kordes (1991) and Meyer (1991) agree that the final stage in the development of interculture would not be the native-like command of the target cultural patterns, but rather the development of an optimal distance from each of these two cultures that allows both the relativisation of the first culture and personal growth. Likewise, Liddicoat (2005) considers that to think in terms of acquisition of a native-like mastery of the target culture creates problems. For example, it is often held that assimilation to the target culture could and should be the aim of language learning. To do so is to reject the significance of identity and cultural attachment and to disregard the fact that any intermediate position could be a way of mediating between two or more cultures.

Kordes (1991) further states that in order to achieve such a degree of interculture, the individual has to experience some type of culture shock which allows them to understand that their existing way of organising experience has to be questioned and that new and unknown ways of coming to terms with reality have to be developed and implemented.

In the transformational model of intercultural competence for professional mobility, interlanguage and interculture are important elements because each individual's interlanguage and interculture are unique and dynamic. However, the relationship between interlanguage and interculture is not simple. Few people would agree with Singerman (1996) that there is a one-to-one correspondence in the development of linguistic and intercultural competences. On the basis of the guidelines offered by the American Council on the Teaching of Foreign Languages, which distinguishes an elementary, intermediate, advanced and superior stage of language development, Singerman (1996: 74-81) establishes an elementary, intermediate, advanced and superior stage of intercultural competence, but in our model there is not necessarily an interdependence between the two.

The intercultural learner is always between languages and cultures and their interlanguage and interculture will be dynamic. Hence, it is possible that individuals who show high proficiency in the target language(s) may not be successful in intercultural interactions. On the contrary, individuals with a limited command of the target language(s) may possess a much higher degree of intercultural competence and be more successful. This model therefore includes a consideration of the complex role interlanguage and interculture play in the process of the development of intercultural competence.

7. Learning-unlearning

7.1 Learning

The development of intercultural competencies, as proposed in the previous section, implies the expansion, the improvement and, above all, the reformulation of competencies previously introduced either in formal or informal education and developed mainly through experiential learning. When people encounter an intercultural experience they already have some social competences that help them to deal with the situation. What we hope and expect will happen through education based on our model is that these competencies will be changed and modified and further developed into intercultural competencies. This process of change through education and training is a fundamental aim of the process of intercultural learning.

As a consequence of formal learning people have concepts of learning which are rooted in the acquisition of knowledge through cognitive development. However, intercultural competence development entails learning from experience both prior to, concurrently with and after formal education. Neither experience nor theoretical knowledge can stand alone. Intercultural experiential learning needs consistent preparation and follow-up in order to be fully achieved. This process of modification of what has already been learned and of the competencies which already exist involves re-evaluating and in some cases discarding what has been learned and taken for granted. This we will call "unlearning". Learning and unlearning is a continuum in intercultural learning, but it is nonetheless a difficult endeavour which requires support and guidance.

Therefore, intercultural learning which takes place formally and informally comprises processes which are articulated and anchored in both theory and practice. We should follow Giroux (2006) in considering that "theory is hardly a luxury connected to the fantasy of intellectual power", instead it is "a resource that enables us to both define and respond to problems as they emerge in particular contexts". Furthermore, the interconnectedness between theory and practice allows the intercultural learner in a lifelong process to "build theory" instead of relying upon anecdotes, isolated experience and overgeneralisation.

7.2 Unlearning

Unlearning involves recognising the validity of other perspectives as part of participation in a democratic society. Furthermore, it offers opportunities for contributing to the radicalisation of democratic life through the formulation of counter-hegemonic positions in society. Dewey and Freire both emphasised the potential of the active side of learning and knowing as well as the reflective side of acting. Both authors highlighted the interconnectedness between experience and reflective thinking and its contribution to democratic life (Dewey, 1956; Freire, 1970). Reflective thinking about experience generates experiential learning. However, there is a need for a pedagogical referent "for understanding the conditions for critical learning and the often hidden dynamics of social and cultural reproduction" and, moreover, this "is the precondition for critical citizenship, social responsibility, and a vibrant and inclusive democracy" (Giroux, 2004: 97). Learning and unlearning are, therefore, methodological and dynamic processes in intercultural competence development which emerge simultaneously and reciprocally from theoretical reflection and experiential learning and contribute to active democracy and citizenship.

Reflective thinking upon experience is therefore an important tool for intercultural development because it makes explicit whatever is implicit in daily routines. Byram introduced and emphasised this aspect of intercultural learning which accounts for the learning-unlearning process, since it is by making explicit the implicit norms, values and attitudes that intercultural agents can initiate a process of becoming aware of underlying principles that rule their routines, of questioning their habits and assumptions and, eventually, of changing them, that is, of learning and unlearning (Byram, 1997).

Dialogue, meaning discursive and communicative interaction, is also an important stimulator of the learning process. In Wink's words, dialogue "moves its participants along the learning curve to that uncomfortable place of relearning and unlearning" (Wink, 1997: 36). In fact, intercultural learning, if the idea of this learning-unlearning-relearning cycle is to be considered, may include some uncomfortable moments of instability and insecurity. However, the challenge which such a dynamic entails can be rewarding, since "unlearning is unpacking some old baggage" (Wink, 1997: 14) and, we would add, enhancing it. This process implies reinterpreting and even discrediting previous knowledge before arriving at another temporary and incomplete stage of knowing.

Due to the fact that intercultural communication and interaction is, to a large extent, unpredictable, intercultural effectiveness is based upon give-and-take exchanges, try-and-escape attempts. It also relies very much on a non-judgemental perspective, although "entirely value-free interpretation" is unlikely to happen (Byram, 1997). This attitude also underlies Ting-Toomey and Chung's concept of a flexible intercultural communicator that they define as one who "is able to make creative connections among cultural values, communication styles and situational issues" (Ting-Toomey and Chung, 2005: 21).

In addition, Ting-Toomey stresses the importance of identity negotiation which she understands as the ability to combine multiple cultural frames of reference when dealing with an intercultural situation (Ting-Toomey, 2005). However, attitudes of adaptability, empathy or flexibility, which are more prone to generate processes of learning, unlearning and relearning, are not without problems. They involve susceptibilities and dignity issues which may cause offence. This is, however, not simply a matter of identity but also of power. Ting-Toomey's face negotiation theory is very helpful here for understanding the subtleties and the dynamics of the learning-unlearning process within intercultural exchange, for the development and intensity of the latter is very much dependent on the success of the former, that is, on "facework negotiation" (Ting-Toomey, 2005). The more the people who interact feel their knowledge is equally valid, the more they learn from each other and the more they make their perspectives available for discussion.

The process of learning, unlearning and relearning in an intercultural exchange reveals intellectual modesty, personal and professional investment and democratic commitment. However, it is not an easily managed one, since it involves not only cognitive growth but also psychological, emotional, civic and ethical unfolding. Nevertheless, although we do not have to totally discard our most cherished values and principles, "we need not be a passive reflector of our biological heritage or our cultural and historical traditions" either (Gardner, 2004: 211) and can still make some room for a change of perspective or, at least, for considering and valuing other perspectives. In order to initiate a learning-unlearning-relearning process of intercultural competence development that is empowering to the individual and to the group, it is essential that it takes the form of a critical pedagogical undertaking which does not ignore the political context of each particular communicative, interactive and participatory exercise. This implies a "critical approach to one's own and other cultural background and a critical view of intercultural interaction" (Phipps and Guilherme, 2004: 3) which gives the intercultural competence development a transformative impulse both to the individual and to society. Such an endeavour may facilitate the justification of beliefs and actions of the self and the other, promote the articulation between both and, furthermore, account for the development of the intercultural competencies envisaged.

8.   Intercultural mobility

8.1   Mobility and culture

Mobility is by no means a new feature of human behaviour. On the contrary, it has given birth and shape to civilisations throughout the times. However, nowadays we feel the need, probably more pressing than ever, to equip citizens with a set of competencies, at both a personal and a professional level, enabling them to fully explore the opportunities of a world that seems to, all of a sudden, have become wide open to them. In this project, we have focused on a set of intercultural competencies which are supposed to help us become interculturally mobile. Why do we bother? Do we not become naturally intercultural by being physically mobile? Why do we dare? Can we be interculturally mobile without being physically mobile?

Mobility has lately been a keyword in transnational programmes both in Europe and beyond. While 2006 was designated by the European Commission as the "European Year of Workers' Mobility", the United Nations Secretary General's Special Representative on International Migration and Development, Peter Sutherland, stated in his speech at the 7th meeting of the Commission on Population and Development that "The world was moving from an era of migration to one of mobility" since "countries were no longer divided strictly into sending and receiving countries, but were increasingly sending, receiving and even transit countries" (Sutherland, 2006). In our view, the difference in terminology – migration and mobility – does not simply address the apparent difference between groups of people moving only one or both ways. It is, we gather, meant to emphasise the underlying perceptions of status, that is, to acknowledge that the groups of people referred to are not only guests but also hosts in a transnational sense. This accounts for the positive connotations of terms such as "expatriates" (or "foreigners" in some languages) and negative connotations of the term "migrants". The attribution of the term "immigrant" to a particular group is influenced not only by the host country's perceptions of the immigrant's country of origin, but also by his/her socioeconomic status. For example, a Portuguese worker going to country X will be seen as an immigrant worker, whereas a Portuguese doctor going to the same country will be seen as a foreign doctor. Such a difference in terminology not only has a great impact on the image (that is, status) of developing countries, in particular, as well as those which have joined the core group of the European Community, but also affects individuals' lives in society in general and, especially, in the workplace. Nevertheless, the common feature of both migrants and expatriates, that is, of all mobile people, is that they are both carriers and producers of culture. They carry their cultural baggage(s), and they adapt, accommodate, resist and create culture, although not in a linear, chronological manner.

8.2 "New" communities of practice

Throughout history people have moved mostly in groups, except for the occasional lone adventurers. With modernity, the development and the ubiquity of new means of transport, new media and new technologies have encouraged individuals to venture further and to move, either virtually or physically, alone or with their families.

However, they do tend eventually to build relations within or settle in communities of individuals who are ethnically and culturally alike. Despite this tendency to converge on such networks, individuals move increasingly across different ethnic communities and cultures, both within and outside their local contexts, both in their private and public spaces. Therefore, individuals move not only across cultures but also on the edge of both the host and the immigrant community as they attempt to construct new communities in their everyday lives, both at work and at home, as well as in-between.

Furthermore, they have personal and professional dreams which are to some extent shared with the host community, although formulated in different ways. At work, all the dynamics of social life are reflected and, at the same time, new relations are created and exported in turn back into social life. New "communities of practice" of "particular collectives" (Rock, 2005: 78) emerge, develop, disappear and may eventually re-emerge or evolve in different directions.

Communities resulting from all types of intercultural mobility, not only cut across the cultural limits of the social and professional structures from which they emerge but also create very particular dynamics, with both positive and negative impulses, among "person[s] in the doing . . . with [their] own 'histories of being' whose 'tensions and conflicts' . . . are resolved, silenced or resisted . . . as the person engages in action and uses the meaning-making mechanisms at her reach" (Keating, 2005). Therefore, intercultural mobility creates a rich and complex holistic process which goes beyond mere displacement, straightforward multicultural interaction or detached cross-cultural communication. As Barton and Tusting (2005) point out "discourse and power are central to understandings of the dynamics of communities of practice".

Thus, from our point of view and bearing our main purpose in mind, the development of intercultural competencies for professional mobility requires not only an awareness of the meaning-making mechanisms and tools available when engaging in cross-cultural action and communication. It is also necessary to develop an ability to manage and explore these mechanisms and tools to achieve "effective" intercultural communication and interaction competence, which are fundamental for living in new and emerging communities and being active citizens in those communities (Guilherme, 2000).

8.3 Intercultural democratic citizenship

When intercultural communication and interaction is "effective" the result is actual intercultural mobility as, despite different motivations, interpretations, strategies and goals, cognition, emotion, action and discourse intermingle in a common task regardless of physical proximity. Furthermore, the importance of the dialogical nature of this both interactive and communicative endeavour has also been recognised at the European level, as the year 2008 was declared "the European Year of Intercultural Dialogue" by the European Parliament. The proposal of the Commission of the European Communities presented to the European Parliament and to the Council states, according to the Lisbon strategy, that "European citizens, and all those living in the Union temporarily or permanently, should therefore be able to acquire the knowledge, qualifications and aptitudes enabling them to deal with a more open, but also more complex, environment . . ." (European Commission, 2005).

Intercultural mobility, as described above, is also only possible when contextualised within a broader project of democratic citizenship, namely the Education for democratic citizenship project (1996 onwards) which was originally set in motion by the Council of Europe and subsequently gave rise to a myriad of projects aiming to develop several different elements, such as "alternative globalisation", "emancipatory multiculturalism" and "multiple citizenships", which contribute to a wider vision of a radical, participatory and "high-intensity" form of democracy (Santos, 2005c).

The model identifies the competences which are necessary to achieve the potential citizenship of living in new and emerging communities. The ICOPROMO project, while attempting to undertake a theoretical and practical journey towards the development of intercultural competencies for professional mobility, engaged us in identifying intercultural competencies that would allow professionals to achieve "effective" intercultural mobility, within the physical, cognitive, emotional, social and ethical dimensions, both in intercultural communication and interaction, within a framework of active democratic citizenship.

8.4 Intercultural competencies for "effective" intercultural mobility

In the previous section, various intercultural competencies for the achievement of intercultural mobility, described as the ability to interact effectively in multicultural professional contexts, were identified and explored (see our model). The "effectiveness" of such an endeavour is, to our understanding, measured by the accomplishment not only of corporate or individual strategic interests through goal-oriented persuasion but also, as previously stated, of reciprocally favourable and respectful negotiation (Guilherme, 2000: 297-300). Furthermore, we endorse the understanding that effectiveness in intercultural communication and interaction refers to the extent to which "mutually shared meaning and integrative goal-related outcomes" are achieved (Ting-Toomey and Oetzel, 2001: 58).

However, as Oetzel argues, it is not only necessary to negotiate the "culturally appropriate definition[s] of group effectiveness" but to clarify whether we are aiming at task or relational effectiveness or both (Oetzel, 2005: 366). Nevertheless, the latter, establishing priorities for effectiveness, depends on the former, the specific cultural definitions of effectiveness. Therefore, in order to be "effectively" responsive to a variety of contexts, as Parmenter (2003: 142; 133) reminds us, it is also important to "relativise accounts of Intercultural Communicative Competence through examining alternative interpretations of concepts relating to self, to language and communication, and to education" as well as to take account of different "national [and individual] responses to the process of globalisation".

In addition, it is paramount to take into consideration the particular response of the individual within the group, as well as that of the group itself, to the intercultural situation within a particular multi- or monocultural social and organisational context while oriented towards the fulfilment of a set, accepted or commonly agreed task. This is the reason why it is commonly agreed that the intercultural professional situation calls for more research on "the constitutive (or creative) role of communication in the creation of group cultures", as well as on "the creation of norms in culturally diverse groups" especially on "how culturally diverse groups utilize the diversity in their groups" (Oetzel, 2005: 368). It is also commonly acknowledged that such meaning-making and relational processes are not value- or power-free and, therefore, even "diversity management initiatives can be seen to perpetuate rather than combat inequalities in the workplace" while "continu[ing] to prescribe essentialist categories of difference and offer problematic dualisms for effecting organizational change" (Lorbiecki and Jack, 2000: 29). Therefore, a main concern of this project was to propose a critical approach, as stated above, to the definition of an "effective" intercultural mobility.

8.5   The intercultural continuum

Intercultural mobility is viewed here as a "horizon", which may be described as Janus-like, that is, it is not only a goal at which we always aim yet never fully reach but also a recurrent starting point. Intercultural mobility entails, therefore, an ontological and epistemological turn where we also look for the other in ourselves. However, the term mobility here, especially if applied to professional settings, can be misleading if understood as to be applied mostly to short-lived and superficial intercultural encounters. On the contrary, following Byram's line of thought, such encounters, even if brief, are only valuable to our study if they aim "to establish and maintain relationships" which, in this project, are not necessarily personal but cannot help being social and professional, rather than aiming at the mere communication of messages and exchange of information or simply direct, detached interaction (Byram, 1997).

In relation to this idea, Byram identifies five main factors, which he calls *savoirs* and which account for the development of intercultural communicative competence, since it is also assumed that they develop within the use of a foreign language. They are:

savoir, savoir comprendre, savoir être, savoir faire and *savoir s'engager* (Byram and Zarate, 1997; Byram, 1997). Although Byram conceptualises the five *savoirs* for the purpose of formal schooling, we believe that they can also be applicable to the development of intercultural competence for professional mobility.

The first factor, *savoir,* refers to new knowledge and specific information one has to acquire, while the second, *savoir comprendre,* refers to a novel perspective of "new" or "old" knowledge. This, we believe, should include formal education in intercultural communication and interaction, therefore, implying the possibility of a new epistemological stance. As far as the third and fourth factors are concerned, *savoir être* and *savoir faire,* they entail an ontological and a methodological change which, in our view, cannot be entirely achieved through experience alone. Finally, the fifth factor, *savoir s'engager,* accounts for full civic and democratic participation. In sum, intercultural mobility is meant firstly to contribute to the establishment and maintenance of relationships and, ultimately, directed towards full participation in different contexts over a period of time.

Intercultural mobility may also be perceived as a frame of mind which allows a cross-cultural encounter to turn into an intercultural one in that it "transforms both parties and which enables both, through languaging, to embark upon new journeys of self and social discovery. It is a journey into intercultural being" (Phipps and Gonzalez, 2004: 22). "Languaging" is a concept appropriately explored by the authors in order to identify a "life skill" since "it is inextricably interwoven with social experience – living in society – and it develops and changes constantly as that experience evolves and changes" (Phipps and Gonzalez, 2004: 2). It implies, therefore, a lengthy process of discovery, of travelling back and forth, of learning and unlearning, of trying, struggling, appreciating and transforming. In sum, intercultural mobility eventually becomes a life journey, that is, "a journey into intercultural being" (Phipps and Gonzalez, 2004: 22).

Intercultural mobility happens across various levels: (a) global, (b) national, (c) local and generates intercultural dialogue between different systems of beliefs, values and attitudes. Any individual can, in principle, 'travel' through these levels, unintentionally, inadvertently and unchanging, yet aware of the differences. That is, this individual can be mobile, have multicultural experiences, perhaps have a pluralistic political position by accepting and enjoying difference, yet never quite reach an intercultural stage as defined above.

It is possible for an individual to accept, enjoy, and live diversity, to adapt and be personally and professionally successful in a multicultural setting. This individual can even live through ontological and epistemological change and, surprisingly, the "engaging" and "languaging" stages. Such an achievement would require her/him to go through "a critical cycle", that is, "a reflective, exploratory, dialogical and active stance towards cultural knowledge and life that allows for dissonance, contradiction, and conflict as well as for consensus, concurrence, and transformation" (Guilherme, 2002: 219).

In addition, this process would entail the experiencing of a series of operations "gathered in three main moments: (a) when one approaches and responds to culture(s) – experiencing, exploring, wondering, and speculating; (b) when one engages with and embarks on (inter)cultural observation, research and interpretation – appreciating, commenting, comparing, reflecting, analysing, and questioning; and (c) when one performs (inter)cultural acts and transforms cultural life – hypothesising, evaluating, negotiating, deciding, *différant*, and acting" (Guilherme, 2002: 221). Such operations should nevertheless require "a cognitive and emotional endeavour that aim[ed] at individual and collective emancipation, social justice and political commitment" (Guilherme, 2002: 219).

Intercultural mobility in the workplace, as we define it and if we are to consider its ontological, epistemological, methodological and civic dimensions, certainly depends on individual vision and commitment, on work group dynamics as well as on organisational structure and culture. However, it is also shaped by a national legal and political framework that is multicultural and stimulates the individual to act as an intercultural citizen (Kymlicka, 2003) and is inspired by counter-hegemonic globalisation which "is animated by a redistributive ethos in its broadest sense, involving redistribution of material, social, political, cultural, and symbolic resources" (Santos, 2005a: 29). In sum, intercultural mobility both demands and stimulates an intercultural ethos at all levels.

9. References

Adler, N., *International Dimensions of Organizational Behavior*, 4th edn Cincinnati, OH, South-Western College Publishing, 1997.

Agar, M., Language Shock: Understanding the Culture of Conversation, New York, William Morrow, 1994a.

Agar, M., "The Intercultural Frame", International Journal of Intercultural Relations, 18 (2), 1994b, pp. 221-237.

Anderson, R.C. and Pearson, P.D., "A Schema-Theoretic View of Basic Processes in Reading Comprehension", in Carrell, P.L., Devine, J. and Eskey, D.E. (eds.), Interactive Approaches to Second Language Reading, Cambridge, Cambridge University Press, 1988.

Anzaldua, G., Borderlands La Frontera, San Francisco, Aunt Lute Books, 1987.

Asante, M.K. and Davis, A., "Encounters in the Interracial Workplace", in Asante, M.K. and Gudykunst, W.B. (eds.), Handbook of International and Intercultural Communication, London, Sage, 1989, pp. 374-391.

Bandura, A., Social Foundations of Thought and Action: A Social Cognitive Theory, Englewood Cliffs, NJ, Prentice Hall, 1986.

Bandura, A., "Self-efficacy", in Ramachaudran, V.S. (ed.), Encyclopedia of Human Behavior, Vol. 4, New York, Academic Press, 1994, pp. 71-81.

Bartlett, C. and Ghoshal, S., Managing Across Borders, Cambridge, MA, Harvard Business School Press, 1998.

Barton, D. and Tusting, K., "Introduction", in Barton, D. and Tusting, K. (eds.), Beyond Communities of Practice: Language, Power, and Social Context, Cambridge, Cambridge University Press, 2005, pp. 1-13.

Bennett, M.J., "Towards Ethnorelativism: A Developmental Model of Intercultural Sensitivity", in Paige, M. (ed.), Education for the Intercultural Experience, Yarmouth, ME, Intercultural Press, 1993a, pp. 21-71.

Bennett, M.J., "Intercultural Communication Styles", unpublished materials from the Summer Institute for Intercultural Communication, Intercultural Communication Institute, Portland, OR, 1993b.

Bennett, M.J. (ed.), Basic Concepts of Intercultural Communication, Yarmouth, ME, Intercultural Press, 1998.

Berlyne, D.E., "Novelty and Curiosity as Determinants of Exploratory behavior", British Journal of Psychology, Vol. 41, 1950, pp. 68-80.

Bhabha, H., The Location of Culture, London, Routledge, 1994.

Brislin, R.W. and Pedersen, P., Cross-cultural Orientation Programs, New York, Gardner Press, Inc., 1976.

Brislin, R.W. and Yoshida, T., Intercultural Communication Training: An Introduction, Thousand Oaks, CA, Sage Publications, 1994.

Brown, H.D., Principles of Language Learning and Teaching, Englewood Cliffs, NJ, Prentice-Hall, 1980 and 1994.

Byram, M., Cultural Studies in Foreign Language Education, Clevedon, Multilingual Matters, 1989.

Byram, M., Teaching and Assessing Intercultural Communicative Competence, Clevedon, Multilingual Matters, 1997.

Byram, M., Gribkova, B. and Starkey, H., Developing the Intercultural Dimension in Language Teaching. A Practical Introduction for Teachers, Strasbourg, Council of Europe Publishing, 2002.

Byram, M., Nichols, A. and Stevens, D. (eds.), Developing Intercultural Competence in Practice, Clevedon, Multilingual Matters, 2001.

Byram, M. and Tost Planet, M. (eds.), Social Identity and the European Dimension: Intercultural Competence Through Foreign Language Learning, Strasbourg, Council of Europe Publishing, 2000.

Byram, M. and Zarate, G., *The Sociocultural and Intercultural Dimension of Language Learning and Teaching*, Strasbourg, Council of Europe, 1997.

Caligiuri, P., "Developing Global Leaders", *Human Resource Management Review*, Vol. 16, No. 2, 2006, pp. 219-228.

Canale, M. and Swain, M., "Theoretical Bases of Communicative Approaches to Second Language Teaching and Testing", *Applied Linguistics*, 1980, Vol. 1, No. 1, pp. 1-47.

Capucho, F., *The Role of Intercomprehension in the Construction of European Citizenship*, Viseu, Universidade Católica Portuguesa, 2002.

Chang, S. and Tharenou, P., "Competencies Needed for Managing a Multicultural Workgroup", *Asia Pacific Journal of Human Resources*, Vol. 42, No. 1, 2004, pp. 57-74.

Cohen, R., "International Conference on Intercultural Communication and Diplomacy – Themes", 2004.

(www.diplomacy.edu/conferences/IC/themes.asp) (visited 18 May 2004)

Commission of the European Communities, "Proposal for a Decision of the European Parliament and of the Council concerning the European Year of Intercultural Dialogue (2008)", 2005.
(http://eur-lex.europa.eu/LexUriServ/site/en/com/2005/com2005_0467en01.pdf) (visited 2 June 2006)

Corder, S.P., *Error Analysis and Interlanguage*, London, Oxford University Press, 1981.

Cui, G. and Awa., N.E., "Measuring Intercultural Effectiveness: An Integrative Approach", *International Journal of Intercultural Relations*, Vol. 16, 1992, pp. 311-328.

Damen, L., *Culture Learning: The Fifth Dimension in the Language Classroom*, Reading, MA, Addison-Wesley Publishing Company, 1987.

Dervin, B., "On Studying Information Seeking and Use Methodologically: The Implications of Connecting Metatheory to Method", *Information Processing and Management*, Vol. 35, 1999, pp. 727-750.

Dewey, J., *Democracy and Education*, New York, Macmillan, 1956 (1st edn, 1916).

DiStefano, J.J. and Maznevski, M.L., "Creating Value with Diverse Teams in Global Management", *Organizational Dynamics*, Vol. 29, No. 1, 2000, pp. 45-63.

Doyé, P., "Intercomprehension. A Guide for the Development of Language Education Policies in Europe: from Linguistic Diversity to Plurilingual Education", Strasbourg, Council of Europe, 2005.
(www.coe.int/t/dg4/linguistic/Source/Doye%20EN.pdf)

Duran, L., "Toward a Better Understanding of Code Switching and Interlanguage in Bilinguality: Implications for Bilingual Instruction", *Journal of Educational Issues of Language Minority Students,* Vol. 14, No. 4, 1994, pp. 69-88.

Earley, P.C. and Ang, S., *Cultural Intelligence: Individual Interactions Across Cultures*, Palo Alto, CA, Stanford University Press, 2003.

Euractiv.com, "NGO: migration is a major poverty risk in Europe", (www.euractiv.com/en/socialeurope/ngo-migration-major-poverty-risk-europe/article-156240) (visited June 2006)

Ferrell, O.C., Fraedrich, J. and Ferrell, L., *Business Ethics: Ethical Decision Making and Cases*, 6th edn, Boston, Houghton Mifflin, 2005.

Festinger, L., *A Theory of Cognitive Dissonance*, Stanford, CA, Stanford University Press, 1957.

Freire, P., *Pedagogy of the Oppressed*, New York, The Continuum, 1970.

Gadamer, H.G., *Truth and Method*, London, Sheed and Ward, 1970.

Giroux, H.A., *Border Crossings: Cultural Workers and the Politics of Education*, New York, Routledge, 1992.

Giroux, H.A., "Is There a Role for Critical Pedagogy in Language/Culture Studies? An Interview with Henry A. Giroux", *Language and Intercultural Communication*, Vol. 6, No. 2, 2006, pp. 163-175 (interviewed by Manuela Guilherme).

Giroux, H.A. and Giroux, S.S., *Take Back Higher Education: Race, Youth, and the Crisis of Democracy in the Post-Civil Rights Era*, New York, Palgrave MacMillan, 2004.

Grünhage-Monetti, M., Halewijn, E. and Holland, C., *ODYSSEUS: Second Language at the Workplace*, Graz/Strasbourg, ECML/Council of Europe, 2003.

Gudykunst, W.B. and Kim, Y.Y., *Communicating with Strangers: An Approach to Intercultural Communication*, New York, Random House, 1984.

Guilherme, M., "Intercultural Competence", in Byram, M. (ed.), *Routledge Encyclopaedia of Language Teaching and Learning*, London, Routledge, 2000, pp. 297-300.

Guilherme, M., *Critical Citizens for an Intercultural World: Foreign Language Education as Cultural Politics*, Clevedon, Multilingual Matters, 2002.

Gusnard, D.A., Ollinger, J.M., Shulman, G.L., Cloninger, C.R., Price, J.L., Van Essen, D.C. and Raichle, M.E., "Persistence and Brain Circuitry", *Proceedings of the National Academy of Sciences of the USA,* Vol. 100, No. 6, 18 March 2003, pp. 3479-3484.

Hall, E.T. , *Beyond Culture*, New York, Doubleday, 1976.

Hall, S., "Introduction: Who Needs Identity?" in Hall, S. and du Gay, P. (eds.), *Questions of Cultural Identity*, London, Sage, 1996.

Hampden-Turner, C. and Trompenaars, F., *Building Cross-cultural Competence: How to Create Wealth from Conflicting Values*, Hoboken, NJ, John Wiley and Sons, Ltd., 2000.

Heyman, S., "The Influence of Cultural Individualism-Collectivism, Self Construals, and Individual Values on Communication Styles across Cultures", *Human Communication Research,* Vol. 22, 1996, pp. 510-543.

Hofstede, G., *Culture's Consequences: International Differences in Work-related Values*, Beverly Hills, CA, Sage Publications, 1980.

Hofstede, G., *Cultures and Organizations: Software of the Mind*, London, McGraw-Hill, 1991.

Huber-Kriegler, M., Lázár, I. and Strange, J., *Mirrors and Windows: An Intercultural Communication Textbook,* Graz/Strasbourg, ECML/Council of Europe, 2003.

Kang, N.-H., *New Patterns of Industrial Globalisation*, OECD, 2001.

Keating, C., "The Person in the Doing: Negotiating the Experience of Self", in Barton, D. and Tusting, K. (eds.), *Beyond Communities of Practice: Language, Power, and Social Context*, Cambridge, Cambridge University Press, 2005, pp. 105-138.

Kim, M.-S., "Constraints as a Tool for Understanding Communication Styles", in Singelis, T.M. (ed.), *Teaching About Culture, Ethnicity and Diversity: Exercises and Planned Activities*, Thousand Oaks, Sage, pp. 101-106.

Kordes, H., "Intercultural Learning at School: Limits and Possibilities", in Buttjes, D. and Byram, M. (eds.), *Mediating Languages and Cultures*, Clevedon, Multilingual Matters, 1991, pp. 287-305.

Kramsch, C., *Context and Culture in Language Teaching*, Oxford, Oxford University Press, 1993.

Kramsch, C., "Identity, Role and Voice in Cross-cultural (mis)Communication", in House, J., Kasper, G. and Ross, S. (eds.), *Misunderstanding in Social Life*, London, Longman, 2003, pp. 129-53.

Kymlicka, W., "Multicultural States and Intercultural Citizens", *Theory and Research in Education*, Vol. 1, No. 2, 2003, pp. 147-169.

Lewin, K., *A Dynamic Theory of Personality*, New York, McGraw-Hill, 1935.

Lewin, K., *Principles of Topological Psychology*, New York, McGraw-Hill, 1936.

Liddicoat, A.J., "Static and Dynamic Views of Culture and Intercultural Language Acquisition, *Babel*, Vol. 36, No. 3, 2002, pp. 4-11, 37.

Liddicoat, A.J., "Teaching Languages for Intercultural Communication", in Cunningham, D. and Hatoss, A. (eds.), *An International Perspective on Language Policies, Practices and Proficiencies*, Fédération Internationale des Professeurs de Langues Vivantes (FIPLV), Belgrave, 2005, pp. 201-214.

Locke, E.A. and Latham, G.P., "Work Motivation: The High Performance Cycle", in Kleinbeck, U., Quast, H.-H., Thierry, H. and Häcker, H. (eds.), *Work Motivation*, Hillsdale, NJ, Lawrence Erlbaum Associates, 1990, pp. 3-25.

Lorbiecki, A. and Jack, G., "Critical Turns in the Evolution of Diversity Management", *British Journal of Management*, Vol. 11, Special Issue, 2000, pp. 17-31.

Marx, E., *Breaking Through Culture Shock: What You Need to Succeed in International Business*, London, Nicholas Brealey, 2000.

McClelland, D.C., *The Achieving Society*, Princeton, NJ, Van Nostrand, 1961.

Meyer, M., "Developing Transcultural Competence: Case Studies of Advanced Foreign Language Learners", in Buttjes, D. and Byram, M. (eds.), *Mediating Languages and Cultures*, Clevedon, Multilingual Matters, 1991, pp. 136-158.

Oetzel, J.G., "Effective Intercultural Workgroup Communication Theory", in Gudykunst, W.B. (ed.), *Theorizing About Intercultural Communication*, Thousand Oaks, Sage, 2005.

Olsson, M., "Sense-Making Methodology: Information Researchers Construct Dervin and Her Work", paper presented at a non-divisional workshop held at the meeting of the International Communication Association, NYC, May 2005. (http://communication.sbs.ohio-state.edu/sense-making/meet/2005/meet05olsson_ex.pdf)

Parmenter, L., "Describing and Defining Intercultural Communicative Competence – International Perspectives", in Byram, M. (ed.), *Intercultural Competence*, Strasbourg, Council of Europe Publishing, 2003, pp. 121-147.

Pencheva, M. and Shopov, T., *Understanding Babel. An Essay in Intercomprehension Analysis*, Sofia, St Kliment Ohridski University Press, 2003.

Pennington, D.L., "Interpersonal Power and Influence in Intercultural Communication", in Asante, M.K. and Gudykunst, W.B. (eds.), *Handbook of International and Intercultural Communication*, London, Sage, 1989, pp. 261-274

Phipps, A. and Gonzalez, M., *Modern Languages: Learning and Teaching in an Intercultural Field*, London, Sage, 2004.

Phipps, A. and Guilherme, M., "Introduction", in Phipps, A. and Guilherme, M., *Critical Pedagogy: Political Approaches to Language and Intercultural Communication*, Clevedon, Multilingual Matters, 2004.

Revell, J. and Norman, S., *In Your Hands. NLP in ELT*, London, Saffire Press, 1999.

Rieder, K., *Intercomprehension in Language Teacher Education*, Vienna, Pädagogische Akademie des Bundes, 2002.

Roberts, C., Byram, M., Barro, A., Jordan, S. and Street, S., *Language Learners as Ethnographers*, Clevedon, Multilingual Matters, 2001.

Rock, F., "I've Picked Some Up from a Colleague: Language, Sharing and Communities of Practice in an Institutional Setting", in Barton, D. and Tusting, K. (eds.), *Beyond Communities of Practice: Language, Power, and Social Context*, Cambridge, Cambridge University Press, 2005, pp. 77-104.

Ronen, S., "Training an International Assignee", in Goldstein, I. (ed.), *Training and Development in Organizations*, San Francisco, Jossey-Bass, 1989, pp. 417-453.

Santos, B. de S., *The World Social Forum: Toward a Counter-hegemonic Globalization*, 2003.

(www.ces.fe.uc.pt/bss/documentos/wsf.pdf) (visited January 2004)

Santos, B. de S., "Reinventing Social Emancipation: Toward New Manifestos", in Santos, B. de S. (ed.), *Democratizing Democracy: Beyond the Liberal Democratic Canon*, London, Verso, 2005a, pp. xvii-xxxiii.

Santos, B. de S., "Beyond Neoliberal Governance: The World Social Forum as Subaltern Cosmopolitan Politics and Legality", in Santos, B. de S. and Rodríguez-Garavito, C.A. (eds.), *Law and Globalization from Below: Towards a Cosmopolitan Legality*, Cambridge: Cambridge University Press, 2005b.

Santos, B. de S. and Avritzer, L., "Introduction: Opening up the Cannon of Democracy", in Santos, B. de S. (ed.), *Democratizing Democracy: Beyond the Liberal Democratic Canon*, London, Verso, 2005c, pp. vii-xxxiii.

Saphiere, D.H., Kappler Mikk, B. and DeVries, B.I., *Communication Highwire, Leveraging the Power of Diverse Communication Styles*, Yarmouth, ME, Intercultural Press, 2005.

Scollon, R. and Scollon, S.W., *Intercultural Communication*, Cambridge, MA, Blackwell, 1995.

Seelye, H.N. and Wasilewski, J.H., *Between Cultures: Developing Self-Identity in a World of Diversity*, Lincolnhood, IL, NTC Publishing Group, 1996.

Seelye, N., *Culture Clash*, Lincolnhood, IL, NTC Business Books, 1995.

Seelye, N. (ed.), *Experiential Activities for Intercultural Learning*, Yarmouth, ME, Intercultural Press, 1996.

Selinker, L., "Interlanguage", *International Review of Applied Linguistics*, Vol. 10, No. 3, 1972, pp. 209-231.

Singerman, A.J., *Acquiring Cross-cultural Competence: Four Stages for American Students of French*, Lincolnhood, IL, National Textbook Company, 1996.

Skutnabb-Kangas, T., *Linguistic Genocide in Education – Or Worldwide Diversity and Human Rights?* London, Lawrence Erlbaum Associates, 2000.

Smith, S.L., Paige, R.M. and Steglitz, I., "Theoretical Foundations of Intercultural Training and Applications to the Teaching of Culture", in Lange, D.L., Klee, C.A., Paige, R.M. and Yershova, Y.A. (eds.), *Culture as the Core: Interdisciplinary Perspective on Culture Teaching and Learning in the Language Curriculum*, Center for Advanced Research on Language Acquisition (CARLA), Working Paper Series, University of Minnesota, 1998.

Stahl, G.K., "Using Assessment Centers as Tools for Global Leadership Development. An Exploratory Study", in Mendenhall, M.E., Kühlmann, T.M. and Stahl, G.K. (eds.), *Developing Global Business Leaders. Policies, Processes and Innovations,* Westport, CT, Quorum Books, 2001, pp. 197-210.

Sutherland, P., *International Migration One of the Great Challenges of the 21st Century*, 2006.

(www.un.org/News/Press/docs//2006/pop946.doc.htm) (visited 2 June 2006)

Szanston, D., "Cultural Confrontation in the Philippines", in Textor, R. (ed.), *Cultural Frontiers of the Peace Corps*, Boston, MA, Massachusetts Institute of Technology Press, 1966, pp. 35-61.

Ting-Toomey, S., *Communicating Across Cultures*, New York, Guilford Press, 1999.

Ting-Toomey, S., "Identity Negotiation Theory: Crossing Cultural Boundaries", in Gudykunst, W.B. (ed.), *Theorizing about Intercultural Communication*, Thousand Oaks, Sage, 2005a, pp. 211-233.

Ting-Toomey, S., "The Matrix of Face: An Updated Face-Negotiation Theory", in Gudykunst, W.B. (ed.), *Theorizing about Intercultural Communication*, Thousand Oaks, Sage, 2005b, pp. 71-92.

Ting-Toomey, S. and Chung, L., *Understanding Intercultural Communication*, Los Angeles, CA, Roxbury, 2005.

Ting-Toomey, S. and Oetzel, J.G., *Managing Intercultural Conflict*, Thousand Oaks, CA, Sage, 2001.

Trompenaars, F., *Riding The Waves Of Culture: Understanding Diversity In Global Business*, Burr Ridge, IL, Irwin Professional Publishing, 1994.

Wall, S. and Rees, B., *International Business*, 2nd edn, New York, Prentice Hall/Financial Times, 2004.

Weick, K.E., *Sensemaking in Organizations*, Newbury Park, CA, Sage, 1996.

Weinrich, U., *Languages in Contact. Findings and Problems*, New York, Publications of the Linguistic Circle of New York, 1953.

Wills, S. and Barham, K., "Being an Intercultural Manager", *European Management Journal*, Vol. 12, No. 1, 1994, pp. 49-58.

Wink, J., *Critical Pedagogy: Notes from the Real World*, New York, Longman, 1997.

Agents de vente des publications du Conseil de l'Europe
Sales agents for publications of the Council of Europe

Council of Europe Publishing/Editions du Conseil de l'Europe
F-67075 Strasbourg Cedex
Tel.: (33) 03 88 41 25 81 – Fax: (33) 03 88 41 39 10 – E-mail: publishing@coe.int – Website: http://book.coe.int